The Watering Place

The Watering Place

LYLE KESSLER

RANDOM HOUSE

 NEW YORK

For Sheila

THE WATERING PLACE *was first presented by Gene Persson and James Walsh on March 12, 1969, at the Music Box, New York City, with the following cast:*

(*In order of appearance*)

MOTHER   Vivian Nathan
JANET   Shirley Knight
FATHER   Ralph Waite
SONNY   William Devane

Directed by Alan Schneider
Setting by Robin Wagner
Lighting by Jules Fisher
Costumes by Jeanne Button
Associate Producer: Rick Hobard

Synopsis of Scenes

ACT ONE

The curtain rises on a living room of a house in an old but still fashionable neighborhood. A solid house, built of strong timber, its foundations are deep in the earth. The house rests on a good-size piece of property, as do all the other houses on the block. They are not row houses . . . one is different from another, built in different years out of different material. Each house has its own history and guards its own secrets. Years ago children played in this neighborhood; today there is no one. The inhabitants remain indoors. Life takes place inside. We never see the outside. The air outside is hot, thick and smoldering. There is a great silence; it is a summer day in July.

The windows on the sides and back of the house are unusually high. They reach to the very top of the house and are shuttered from the sun. Its rays slip through, casting slivers of light about the periphery of the room. A staircase up center leads to the second floor and is covered with a brown carpet. Downstage is a large green area rug . . . on it a sofa, rocker, chairs, tables, lamps . . . a small lit living area surrounded by emptiness . . . and beyond that, furniture, books, pictures, antiques, everything dimly perceived and in shadow and casting shadows of its own. The room is composed of browns and greens, shadow and light. It is not a cluttered, but rather a comfortable and thoroughly lived-in room.

MOTHER, *in a black dress, an open Bible on her lap, has fallen asleep in her chair. Next to her on a table is a small lamp which is softly lit. One other lamp may be on.*

JANET *has opened a few slats of a shutter and is looking out a side window. She is wearing a maternity dress.* JANET *is nine months pregnant.*

MOTHER *is just waking up.*

MOTHER   I must have dozed off. I haven't done that in years. I was reading the Bible and I dozed off. (JANET *remains at the window, looking out*) It must be the weather. (*Pause*) Do you have the time, Janet?

JANET   No, I don't.

MOTHER   Isn't that a watch you're wearing?

JANET   I have no watch.

MOTHER   Around your neck, I mean. Isn't that a watch around your neck?

JANET   It is a watch. I never use it though. I never wind it.

MOTHER   Ronald gave that to you, didn't he?

JANET   It was a birthday gift.

MOTHER   I remember. It was shortly before you were married. Ronald asked my advice. It was between that

4

and a gold brooch. I preferred the watch. It's more practical. (*Pause*) Of course, if you never wind it, it might just as well have been the gold brooch. (*Pause*) Is there any sign of Father?

JANET   No. The street is deserted.

MOTHER   What is so fascinating about an empty street?

JANET   The sun is boiling the tar on the road.

MOTHER   Really?

JANET   Yes, it's almost liquid.

MOTHER   Imagine that! (*Pause*) We were smart not to go to church today.

MOTHER   Father should be home too. He can never let a Sunday go by. He's too old for the games he plays. (*Pause*) It's nice in here though, don't you think? It's cool with the shutters closed.

JANET   The air is stale.

MOTHER   Stale?

JANET   Yes, it's not fresh.

MOTHER   I never noticed that.

JANET   The windows are never opened. We breathe in the same foul air, day in and day out.

MOTHER   I can't open the windows on a day like today.

JANET   They haven't been opened all summer.

MOTHER   If I opened just one window, the cool air would escape and the hot air rush in. The house would become unbearable. (*Pause*) I'm comfortable in here. I'm surprised you're not. (*Pause*) Of course, you have all that activity inside you. All that pressure. (*Pause*) Is he very active today?

JANET   No. No more than usual.

MOTHER   He's a calm one, all right. When I was pregnant with Ronald, he tried to kick his way out. I think this one likes it just where he is. (*Church bells ring*) It must be noon. The service is over. (*Pause*) Why don't you adjust your watch? (*Pause*) Janet, do you hear me? It's noon! Why don't you wind your watch? (JANET *winds the watch*) If the grandfather clock was working there would be no need to ask the time of day.

JANET   I love that grandfather clock.

MOTHER   It stopped working when Ronald was a little boy.

JANET   I fell in love with it the first time I came here.

MOTHER   It'll be yours someday, Janet. Everything will! (JANET *walks over and touches it. She touches the other objects in the house*) I wonder what the sermon was today. (*Pause*) I'm sure we didn't miss anything though.

I don't like that new minister. I don't like the sound of his voice.

JANET   What's wrong with it?

MOTHER   He sounds as if he has phlegm in his throat. I always expect him to cough up a piece when he's reading from the Scriptures.

JANET   He does sound as if he has a frog in his throat.

MOTHER   Phlegm! Not a frog, phlegm! I wouldn't mind so much if it was a frog . . . but phlegm! It's disgusting! I get more out of reading to myself, here in the house, than at the service. Reverend Rhodes was different. I never missed a Sunday. No one did. People came from miles to hear him. We had the biggest congregation in the neighborhood in those days. What are you doing?

JANET   Dusting.

MOTHER   I dusted this morning.

JANET   I know. I enjoy it though. This feather duster is so light.

MOTHER   Why don't you sit down, Janet. Rest! You shouldn't be up and about like that.

JANET   I can't sit all day. I'm perfectly healthy. There's no reason for me not to be up.

MOTHER (*At the window*) Not a sign of him.

JANET It's early, Mother. There's nothing to worry about. The game isn't half over.

MOTHER A man his age, playing ball! In this weather! Do you realize he's an old man? He's retired.

JANET He's strong though. I don't know a man his age that strong.

MOTHER He's not so strong in bed. He acts his age there. It's only in the daytime he's strong. At night he complains about every ache and pain and I have to rub him down. (*Pause*) Janet, sit down! You're making me nervous. I dusted there already. (JANET *sits*) Are you hungry?

JANET No.

MOTHER You left your whole breakfast.

JANET I wasn't hungry.

MOTHER I don't understand it.

JANET I can't eat much in this weather.

MOTHER You have to, for the baby. It has to have its strength.

JANET It has strength.

MOTHER When I was pregnant with Ronald, I was ravenous. You have an appetite like a bird.

JANET It's the weather.

MOTHER You don't even eat enough to sustain one person.

JANET I'm not starving.

MOTHER That's why the baby never kicks.

JANET It kicks.

MOTHER (*Going to her*) Let me feel it.

JANET (*Moving away*) Mother, please!

MOTHER Why won't you let me feel it kick?

JANET I don't like to be touched.

MOTHER When I was pregnant, I let everyone touch me. I was proud to be a mother. It's an act of God!

JANET I just don't want to be fingered. It has nothing to do with you. I don't want *anyone* touching me.

MOTHER I'm his grandmother!

JANET I'm his mother!

MOTHER   Ronald is dead now. I have no one else.

JANET   I'm sorry, Mother. It just makes me nervous.

MOTHER   I won't touch you then. I'll keep my hands behind my back. (*She puts them behind her*) Let me put
my ear to your stomach. I just want to listen to him. I
want to make sure he's alive.

JANET   He's alive!

MOTHER   Where are you going?

JANET   Upstairs.

MOTHER   I won't bother you. Don't go up.

JANET   I'm tired, Mother. I'm suddenly very tired. It's a
hot day. I just want to rest.

MOTHER   You can rest down here. Stay, Janet. Keep me
company.

   (*Sound of a key in the door*)

JANET   There's Father. He'll keep you company. I want to
lie down.

   (JANET *disappears upstairs.* MOTHER *remains at
   the foot of the stairs.* FATHER *comes in. He has spike
   shoes tied around his neck and carries an old
   fielder's mitt which he punches from time to time
   to punctuate his remarks*)

FATHER   What's the talk?

MOTHER What talk?

FATHER What's all the talk about?

MOTHER There's no talk.

FATHER I heard talk.

MOTHER No one's talking. Janet's upstairs resting.

FATHER It's a bitch of a day!

MOTHER You have no business being outside.

FATHER I'm soaked to the skin!

MOTHER Take off that sweatshirt.

FATHER I pitched three innings out there . . . three innings in this heat and then they call the game. The bastards! Can you imagine that! I could have gone the distance. I mean, I had my stuff. They couldn't touch me . . . none of them. They have no stamina. The bastards! I could have gone the distance and then some. I had my stuff! I had my stuff today!

(*He keeps punching his glove*)

Blackout

Ten minutes later. The room is empty. FATHER *is upstairs in the shower, singing and humming. "When the Red, Red, Robin Comes Bob, Bob, Bobbin' Along . . ." The door opens. A figure is silhouetted by the sun. He closes the door. It is a young man wearing an army outfit . . . open shirt, pants and combat boots. Over his shoulder he carries a duffel bag. He stands still and listens as* FATHER *continues to sing.*

He walks through the room, looking around. He stops at the stairs, puts his bag down and listens.

FATHER *enters from the kitchen. She sees him and stops.* MOTHER *hums and sings in the background.*

MOTHER   How did you get in here?

SONNY   The door was open. I walked in.

MOTHER   My husband is upstairs!

(FATHER *is heard singing*)

SONNY   Yes. I hear him. When I was outside and heard him singing I said to myself, this is it . . . I'm here . . . I'm finally home!

MOTHER   Who are you?

SONNY   Sonny. (*Pause*) Sonny's my name. I know who you are. I know all about you. You're Ronald's mother!

MOTHER   You know Ronald?

SONNY   I knew him. Yes.

MOTHER (*She walks closer*)   Ronald was a prisoner of war.

SONNY   We were both prisoners of war. We were in the same stinking mess together. (*Pause*) Do you mind if I sit down? I'm still a little weak.

MOTHER   I'm sorry. Sit down. (*He sits on the sofa*) You must be exhausted. It's so hot out.

SONNY   I'm used to the heat. Where I come from . . . where I just came from, the heat is unbearable.

MOTHER   Can I get you something?

SONNY   No thank you. (*Pause*) It's *tropical* . . . where I come from it's *tropical*. It's hot here, I'm not denying that, but it's not *tropical*. You spend some time in the tropics and you learn to stand any degree of heat.

MOTHER   Ronald couldn't stand hot weather. It was the extremes that bothered him.

SONNY   Do you know, this city is deserted. There's not a soul out there. Not one person to ask the time of day.

13

It's lucky I knew my way. Ronald gave me explicit directions.

MOTHER   He did?

SONNY   I'm glad I had them, believe you me. I'm glad I had those directions. I was blinded momentarily. There was a duststorm and I was blinded. I know it's hard to believe, but out there, right beyond the city, a storm is raging.

MOTHER   I can believe that. It's a summer storm. The other day it was pouring in the front, and out back the sun was shining. (*Pause*) You'll stay for dinner, won't you?

SONNY   Yes. I would like that. I would like to have dinner with Ronald's family.

MOTHER   You'll have to spend some time with us. There's so little we know.

SONNY   I'll be glad to fill you in.

MOTHER   We know Ronald was a prisoner of the war. We had known that for months . . . that he was in a prisoner-of-war camp.

SONNY   Not a camp exactly. More of a village. Actually it was a hut.

MOTHER   We expected him home. They were planning an exchange of prisoners.

SONNY   I know all about that exchange of prisoners. One major for another major. There were three of us in that hut . . . three prisoners, that's all it would hold, the major, Ronald and I. Then there was only Ronald and I.

MOTHER   I was afraid he called for me. That's what I can't get out of my mind. That he called for me and I wasn't there.

SONNY (*Standing*)   I was there though! Don't you worry! He was in good hands! (*He walks to the window*) This is a lovely neighborhood. Each house has a lawn. That's nice. Where I grew up you never saw any green. (*Pause*) Your house needs a coat of paint.

MOTHER   Paint?

SONNY   Yes, it could do with a coat.

MOTHER   I hadn't noticed. I don't get out much any more.

SONNY   One coat. That's enough. Spread it thin.

(*Walks across the room to the stairs*)

MOTHER   I've stayed at home since Ronald died. I prefer to be in. I don't even go to church any more. You would think he was the only soldier who ever died, the way they stare at us. I feel their eyes on the back of my neck through the whole service. They have no manners! When Janet and I walk down the aisle, every head in the church turns.

(SONNY *is looking up the stairs*)

SONNY   He's finished his shower.

MOTHER   Father?

SONNY   Yes. Why don't you call him.

MOTHER (*Gets up*)   I will. I want him to meet you.

SONNY   And I want to meet him. I've been looking forward to meeting him.

MOTHER (*Goes to the foot of the stairs and calls*)   FATHER!

(*There is no answer.* MOTHER *goes upstairs.* SONNY *goes to the rocker. He touches it softly, then rocks it once or twice. He sits on it and rocks*)

FATHER (*Offstage*)   WHAT! (FATHER *appears at the head of the stairs, naked, except for a towel around his waist*) Who is that? (*Pause*) Who is that in my rocker?

MOTHER (*Appears*) I told you who he was.

FATHER   What's he doing in my rocker?

MOTHER   I don't know.

FATHER   Get him off!

(MOTHER *comes down to the couch*)

MOTHER   Sonny! Sit over here! It's much more comfortable!

(SONNY *gets up and goes to the couch. He sits down.*
FATHER *comes down the stairs*)

FATHER   How did he get in here?

MOTHER   I was in the kitchen. When I came in he was
here.

FATHER (*Goes to his rocker and stands behind it, holding
it*)   I told you to keep that door locked. I warned you.
This is what happens when the door is left open.

MOTHER   You were the last one in, Father. You left it
open.

FATHER   You trust the world. I don't. I've been around. I
know the kind of animal that walks this planet. Anything
could walk through that door. I just don't mean a thief.
That's the least of it. There's violence out there. You
haven't been in contact with it, I have. A pervert could
walk in here! A murderer even!

MOTHER   He's just a soldier.

FATHER   What makes you think he's a soldier? The
khakis? The boots? That outfit isn't hard to come by.

MOTHER   He was a prisoner of war. He was with Ronald.

FATHER (*Sitting in his rocker*)   Is that a fact?

MOTHER   Yes.

FATHER   I wasn't asking you. I was asking him. (*Pause*)
I was asking him if it was a fact. (*Pause*) Is it a fact?

SONNY   Yes.

FATHER   You and Ronald were together?

SONNY   That's right.

FATHER   You're a soldier, huh? (SONNY *nods*) Did a little
fighting, huh? (*He nods again*) How was it over there?
Rough?

SONNY   Not too bad.

FATHER   You can take it, huh?

SONNY   I get along.

FATHER   Good! That's what I like to hear . . . a man
after my own heart! (*Pause*) What did you say your
name was?

SONNY   Sonny.

FATHER (*Takes out a cigar*)   Smoke?

SONNY   No, thank you.

FATHER (*Lighting it*)   Do you mind if I smoke?

SONNY   No.

18

FATHER   No vices, huh?

SONNY   Some. Smoking isn't one of them.

MOTHER   Why don't you go upstairs and put on some clothes?

FATHER   I'm comfortable.

MOTHER   You're naked!

FATHER   So what? He's a soldier, isn't he? He can take it!

MOTHER   Janet may come down.

FATHER   She can take it too!

MOTHER   Father!

FATHER   There's nothing wrong with flesh. There's nothing wrong with what God gave us.

SONNY   How is Janet?

FATHER   What's it to you?

MOTHER   He's just asking.

FATHER   What's it to him how she is? What the hell is it his business?

MOTHER   He has manners. That's more than I can say for you. He's not standing around naked.

FATHER   I have a towel.

MOTHER   Put on your clothes!

FATHER   I'll wear my robe.

MOTHER (*Pause*)   Well?

FATHER   I'm not leaving you alone with him.

MOTHER   Why not?

FATHER   I don't trust him.

MOTHER   I trust him!

FATHER   If you want me to wear my robe, you'll have to get it. I'm staying right here and keeping my eye on him.

(MOTHER *goes upstairs.* FATHER *speaks after she is out of sight*) What did you say to her?

SONNY   What do you mean?

FATHER   You say anything to her?

SONNY   About what?

FATHER   You be careful what you say in front of that woman. Understand? She's under a strain. She lost her child. Her only son. Ronald! We don't have visitors here. They upset her.

SONNY   I don't want to upset her. That's the last thing I have in mind.

FATHER   You keep your mouth shut, we'll get along. Understand? Mum's the word!

SONNY   I understand.

FATHER   You have any questions . . . anything bothers you . . . you come to me. I'll take care of it. That woman means the world to me. She's my whole life. (MOTHER *comes down with the bathrobe. Softly*) Mum's the word.

SONNY   Mum's the word.

MOTHER   Here! (*She holds robe open for him. He slips into it*) I don't know why you won't get dressed.

FATHER   I'm comfortable in my robe. It's relaxing. (*Pause*) I played some ball this morning. I like to shower and slip on my robe afterwards.

MOTHER   No one walks around like that.

FATHER   I play every Sunday. It keeps me trim. It keeps me on my toes. Then I top it off with a nice hot steaming shower. Makes me feel alive . . . gets the blood running . . . the body tingling. You know what I mean? I'm in tiptop shape! I wish it had been me instead of Ronald in that P-O-W camp. There would have been a possibility of survival then. With me, there would have been a chance, a good chance, with Ronald, none. He could never rise to the occasion.

MOTHER   He was a sick child. Ronald was always short of breath.

FATHER   I never expected the army to take him. I never expected him to pass the physical.

MOTHER   Sonny's going to fill us in about everything.

FATHER   There's no point opening old wounds.

MOTHER   Sonny was there!

FATHER   I'm not interested.

MOTHER   You may not be interested, but I am.

FATHER   Soldiers are killed in wartime. That's the nature of war.

MOTHER   I want to hear about it!

FATHER   You want to hear about it? I'll tell you about it. I was in a war or two in my time. I know what it's all about. I was in the big ones. Christ, I remember those days. The First War. The first big global conflict. I was a kid then. I was hardly out of knickers. I lied about my age. They took me. I was a big kid. I was mature for my age. In those years we grew up fast. We weren't pampered. Nobody powdered our asses. I fought in the first big one. That was in the trenches. Not like the Second War. We were all over the place then. We moved all over the whole damn map of Europe in the Second World War. In that First War . . . in that first big one, we stayed put. I spent years in a trench—they finally pulled me out. I got a dose of mustard gas and they had to haul my ass out of there. I was trim in those days. War keeps you trim. Now I play ball. On Sunday. That's how I keep in shape. Feel my gut. (*Pause*) Go ahead! Grab ahold! (SONNY *makes an effort*) Nothing to catch hold of, huh? You know how old I am? (*Pause*) Guess!

SONNY   Fifty?

FATHER   Ha! Guess again!

SONNY   Fifty-five?

FATHER   Wrong! Sixty-seven! I'm sixty-seven years old and I have no gut. You ever see a man my age with no gut? I'm solid as a rock!

MOTHER   It's nothing to brag about.

FATHER   It's nothing, huh? I'm the envy of the neighborhood. The other men my age look like tottering old fools . . . those overstuffed baboons! Their bones creak when they walk.

MOTHER   Why don't you act your age?

FATHER You want me to be a bent-up old fart, like those other bent-up old farts?

MOTHER I want you to act your age. You're sixty-seven years old.

FATHER I pitch nine innings of ball every Sunday. Hardball! Not softball! I have a world of experience behind me. They'd like to be in my shoes . . . all of them, even the young ones. I have what it takes. Finesse! That's the secret. I keep 'em guessing. They can't touch me. I throw them my knuckler, my screwball . . . I mix 'em up . . . I throw them my curve. I outfox the lot of them! (*Pause*) You play ball?

SONNY Some.

MOTHER Sonny is staying for dinner.

FATHER When I was your age I pitched a doubleheader, one game after another, and thought nothing of it.

MOTHER I don't know if we have anything in the house. I better look in the freezer. (MOTHER *goes into the kitchen*)

FATHER They don't have what it takes today. They can't even last a game . . . a few innings, that's all . . . a few innings and they're under the shower. (*Pause*) What are your plans?

SONNY Plans?

FATHER You have plans, don't you?

SONNY Not really.

FATHER You have no plans?

SONNY Well, I might reenlist. I haven't decided. I haven't made up my mind yet. After I've had a good long rest, I might sign up for another tour of duty. They offer a bonus, you know.

FATHER The reason I ask is if you happen to be in the city next Sunday, if you just happen to be around, give me a ring, I'll take you out to the game.

SONNY If I happen to be around I just might take you up on that.

FATHER I took Ronald with me. When he was a kid he was magnificent. He bagged flys like a pro. When he was only four and five he had the makings of a future Ty Cobb.

SONNY He thought a lot of you too. He thought a lot of his father.

FATHER He talked about me, huh?

SONNY Your name was never far from his lips.

FATHER Well, he was my son. Ronald was the only child I ever had.

SONNY   You set a fine example.

FATHER   I did my best. I taught him everything I know. I showed him how to oil his glove . . . how to break it in just right. All the tricks of the trade.

SONNY   Not all of it was peaches and cream, of course. What is? Nothing in this world is one hundred per cent peaches and cream.

   (*A pause*)

FATHER   What do you mean by that?

SONNY   Well, we have our ups and then we have our downs.

FATHER   What the hell are you talking about?

SONNY   The world is composed of ups and downs.

FATHER   You double-talking me? (*Pause*) What the hell kind of double-talk is that? . . . Ups! Downs! Peaches! Cream!

MOTHER (*Offstage*)   WE DON'T HAVE A THING IN THE HOUSE!

FATHER   You and Ronald must have been on a talking spree.

MOTHER   (*Enters*) You'll have to take me shopping, Father.

26

FATHER   You must have had yourselves a regular gab-fest.

SONNY (*Stands up*)   That reminds me! I did a little shopping myself on the way over. (*Walks over to his duffel bag*) Nothing special, you understand. I didn't have the time for it. I only had enough time to shop for Janet. (*Brings the bag back to the couch*) Don't worry though! I'll get around to the two of you. I haven't forgotten you.

MOTHER   That's not necessary.

SONNY   I wouldn't think of coming empty-handed. (SONNY *pulls out a large package. He hands it to* MOTHER) I hope she likes it.

MOTHER   I'm sure she will. (MOTHER *goes to the stairs. She calls*) JANET!

FATHER   Leave her be!

MOTHER   What's the matter with you?

FATHER   She's fine where she is!

MOTHER   I want her to meet Sonny.

FATHER   She can do without him! She can get along just fine without him!

(MOTHER, *obstinately, turns and calls again*)

MOTHER   JANET, DO YOU HEAR ME?

JANET (*Offstage*)   Yes, I hear you. (FATHER *angrily walks*

to the side of the room and watches SONNY. *He doesn't take his eyes off him during the scene.* JANET *appears*)
I fell asleep.

MOTHER We have company.

JANET Company?

MOTHER Yes. A friend of Ronald's. A soldier.
(SONNY *stands up and she sees him*)

JANET Oh!

MOTHER Come down.

JANET (*Turns away*) I just got up. My hair's a mess.

MOTHER That's all right. Don't stand on ceremony.
(JANET *has walked offstage*) JANET! COME DOWN HERE! (JANET *reappears slowly. She walks self-consciously down the steps.* SONNY *stares at her in amazement. He turns to* FATHER, *half smiles, and turns back to* JANET. JANET *stops at the bottom of the stairs*) This is Sonny. He was in prison with Ronald.

(*A pause*)

SONNY Hello, Janet.

JANET Hello.

MOTHER Sonny brought you this.
(*She hands her the package*)

JANET Thank you.

(SONNY *walks over to her*)

SONNY It's a dress, Janet. I'm afraid it won't fit though. I wasn't aware of your condition. I was in the wrong department. I was in the Junior Miss Department when I should have been in the Maternity Department.

FATHER I'm thirsty!

MOTHER I forgot to tell you Janet was pregnant.

SONNY Yes, I noticed that.

MOTHER I forgot you wouldn't know about it.

SONNY Ronald never mentioned it.

MOTHER How could he? Ronald never knew. He was shipped overseas.

SONNY That's too bad.

MOTHER We wrote him, but he never received the letters. He was a prisoner already. They returned the letters, unopened.

SONNY Ronald would have been pleased to know his life was in a sense . . . perpetuated. That there would be life coming after him.

MOTHER I don't know how I could have forgotten that.

FATHER   I said I was thirsty! (*Pause*) Well!

MOTHER   What do you want?

FATHER   Water!

MOTHER   Sonny?

SONNY   Water's fine.

MOTHER   I have lemonade. There's a whole pitcher of lemonade.

SONNY   Good.

MOTHER   Janet?

JANET   I'm not thirsty.

MOTHER   Lemonade, Father?

FATHER   Water!

   (MOTHER *leaves*)

SONNY   Why don't you open your present, Janet?

JANET   There's no point. Isn't that what you said? It won't fit me in my condition.

FATHER   Janet, go in and help mother. (JANET *leaves.* FATHER *goes over to the duffel bag and gives it a kick*) What else is in there?

SONNY Just some odds and ends.

(FATHER *nudges it with his foot so that a few items fall out*)

FATHER Odds and ends, huh?

SONNY Yes. Army paraphernalia.

FATHER Move them out of here! They're stinking up the living room! (*Pause*) Get your stinking odds and ends out of here! (SONNY *goes to the bag, bends and stuffs the items back.* FATHER, *behind him, watches a moment, then grabs him in a neckhold*) What's your game, buster? What's eating you?

SONNY You're choking me.

FATHER I'll choke the life out of you, you hear! I told you to keep your mouth shut. I told you mum was the word! I don't want that woman upset. I want you out of here. Understand? You're not staying for dinner. You're checking out now. (FATHER *tightens his grip.* SONNY *moans*) Do you understand me?

SONNY (*Half audible, still being choked*) Yes.

FATHER You do what I say?

SONNY Yes.

FATHER When they come back I'll feed you the line. I'll say Sonny has something to say. Then you tell them you have to get going. You have to catch a train. Stay seated until then. Keep your mouth shut. (JANET *appears in the doorway with a glass of water. She stops and watches.* FATHER *pushes* SONNY *to the sofa.* SONNY *sits there gasping for breath.* JANET *hands* FATHER *the water)* Thank you, Janet. (*Takes a sip*) This hits the spot.

(JANET *sits down.* MOTHER *carries in a tray with a pitcher and three glasses*)

MOTHER This has been a terrible summer. The heat's oppressive. (*Pours three glasses*) This was Ronald's favorite drink. It's a combination of lemon and lime. (*Hands a glass to* SONNY *and then one to* JANET. MOTHER *sits down with a glass*) When he was a little boy he would mix a big batch of it in a bucket and sell it from his wagon. Five cents a cup! Everyone drank from that same cup!

FATHER It's a lousy drink, lemonade! It's too sweet. It never quenched my thirst. This is the thirst quencher. Water. Pure spring water.

MOTHER Lemonade is refreshing in the summer.

FATHER When I was a boy this was open fields. There was no city then. It was all open fields and trees. There were animals, too. Not the tamed kind . . . not this domestic shit . . . pussycats and doggies. I mean animals! The kind you never pet. There was a spring, too. A stream. They filled it in and plugged it up. It still runs though, I still fill my jug with it every week. It's only a trickle now, only a shadow of its former self.

In those days I would bend down and drink my fill, just like God intended me to, right from the stream.

(*A pause*)

MOTHER   Sonny, you haven't touched your drink.

FATHER   They plugged it up, goddamn them, they cut the trees, leveled the land and filled in the stream. They civilized the place! It was beautiful here then. It was a paradise. They could never get rid of that stream though, not altogether; they filled it in one place, it popped up another. That's power! You don't write that off so easily. You can't keep all that pressure plugged up. It has to burst out somewhere. It has to come to the surface somehow. (*Stands up*) I think I'll have another. (*Walks toward the kitchen with his empty glass. He stops at the couch, behind* SONNY) You won't have any shopping to do after all, Mother.

MOTHER   Yes I will. I need a roast.

FATHER   I'm afraid you're not having company for dinner.

MOTHER   What do you mean?

FATHER   What's-his-name can't make it. (*Pause.* MOTHER *looks at* SONNY) What did you say your name was?

MOTHER   His name is Sonny. You know that.

FATHER   It slipped my mind. I was never good on names. Anyway, Sonny here has to catch a train. It's unfortunate, but he has to go cross-country. Isn't that right?

SONNY I have to catch a train.

MOTHER You said you would stay for dinner.

SONNY I forgot. My train is leaving now. I forgot all about it.

    (SONNY *gets up*)

MOTHER I thought you would spend some time with us.

SONNY (*Picks his bag up*) I have to go. I'm sorry.

FATHER He'll come back some other time, Mother. Maybe he'll even spend a week with us.

    (SONNY *has started for the door. He walks slowly, hesitantly, his body begins to shake and he falls to the floor*)

MOTHER Oh!

SONNY I'm all right. It's nothing. It's just weakness. (*Tries to get up and falls again*) They threw us slops. Like pigs. I'm still weak. I don't have my full strength back.

    (MOTHER *goes to him and helps him up*)

MOTHER You're not going anywhere in this condition. You go upstairs and rest.

FATHER He has to catch a train!

    (SONNY *falls again*)

34

MOTHER Oh, my God!

FATHER He'll miss his train!

MOTHER He's not going anywhere!

FATHER He has a train to catch!

MOTHER He's staying right here! I won't let him leave like this. He'll stay right here until he gets all his strength back.

> (SONNY *tries to get up, makes it only halfway and falls again*)

SCENE 3

One hour later. JANET, *alone on the couch, is unwrapping* SONNY's *present. She takes out a dress, a low-cut form-fitting dress. She holds it up and looks at it. She goes to a mirror and holds it in front of her.* SONNY *appears at the top of the stairs and watches her.*

SONNY   Do you like that shade? (JANET, *startled, folds the dress and puts it back in the box.* SONNY *comes down*) The salesgirl said it was a neutral. You can get more use out of a neutral shade, she told me. It's not limited by its color.

JANET   I thought you were sick.

SONNY   I recuperated.

JANET   I thought you were too weak to stand.

SONNY   I have extraordinary recuperative powers. That's what the doctors tell me. When I got out of prison they examined me for a week. They gave me a thorough going-over! They pulled my clothes off! They stripped me down! One doctor called another doctor and eventually the whole staff was over me, a whole platoon of doctors, all in their clean white hospital robes, each one pushing the other to get a better look. There was

36

almost a stampede! I was almost trampled! What would Hippocrates say . . . I ask you that . . . what would he say if he could see the way they were poking and probing at me, pinching and pulling, grabbing my bare flesh? He wouldn't be happy, I can tell you that much. Hippocrates would have frowned upon such a display! (*Pause*) They never came upon anyone like me before . . . I realize that! . . . I do take that into consideration! (*Pause*) I must be an amazing specimen! (*Pause*) Where is everyone?

JANET   Shopping.

SONNY   Shopping?

JANET   They left a few minutes ago.

(*A pause*)

SONNY   Then we're alone.

JANET   Yes.

SONNY   Fancy that!

(*A pause*)

JANET   They won't be gone very long. Mother is just picking up a few things for dinner.

SONNY   Do you know how long it's been since I've been alone with a girl? I mean, a woman? I don't remember how to behave. How about giving me some pointers, Janet? How do we get started? What do I do?

(*A pause*)

JANET Why did you come here?

SONNY I promised Ronald. When it was obvious that he would never come back, he made me promise. Ronald thought it would bring a certain amount of comfort to his family, knowing I was with him.

(*A pause*)

JANET What did he say about me?

SONNY Ronald?

JANET Yes.

SONNY He spoke of you often.

JANET What did he say?

SONNY He described you. He described you in detail. (*Pause*) Of course, he was unaware of the latest development. This new addition is a surprise. I must say it startled me. I don't surprise easily. I'm usually ahead of the game, if you know what I mean. But when I saw you at the head of the stairs filled to the gills . . . I was speechless.

(*A pause*)

JANET Do you think it'll be a boy?

SONNY One or the other.

38

JANET Mother thinks so. Mother thinks it can't be anything else but a boy. She plans to call it Ronald.

SONNY Ronald?

JANET Yes.

SONNY Ronald? Why not? That's perfect! I can't think of a better name.

JANET She says he'll have blond hair and blue eyes, just like Ronald. She thinks I'm going to give birth to an angel.

SONNY That's normal. Grandmothers are like that. (*Pause*) He may not have those exact characteristics though. The blond hair and blue eyes, I mean. It depends on the circumstances. He may have other secondary characteristics.

JANET What do you mean?

(*A pause*)

SONNY (*Shaking his head*) I never would have thought it of you, Janet.

JANET What are you suggesting? (*Pause*) Are you suggesting this is not Ronald's child?

SONNY If it is, it's long overdue. Well-baked, I would say!

JANET This is Ronald's baby.

SONNY Let's face facts, Janet. Ronald left fifteen months ago. It's been about fifteen months since Ronald's been home. I mean, I'm not a mathematician, I excelled in other areas, math wasn't one of them, but I *can* do a little addition and subtraction. I *can* add two and two, and according to my calculations, this baby is six months late. That's stretching it a bit . . . wouldn't you say?

JANET It's Ronald's!

SONNY There are some warm-blooded animals that have longer gestation periods . . . I'm aware of that, I was taught that in biology, but man isn't one of them, man doesn't fit in that category of mammals.

JANET If it's not Ronald's child, whose is it?

SONNY I don't know. I have no idea. You tell me. Isn't that your department? You tell me who knocked you up.

JANET RONALD!

SONNY You been fucking around, Janet. Is that what you've been doing, fucking around? (*Pause*) While Ronald was rotting away in prison you been fucking around, huh? (*Pause*) Don't get me wrong. I don't look down on that particular activity. If you been fucking around, that's your business. Just don't try to put one over on me.

JANET This is Ronald's baby. It has his personality. His intelligence.

SONNY   Come off it!

JANET   Want to feel him?

SONNY   Not particularly.

JANET   (*Goes to him*)   Go on. Give him a squeeze.

SONNY   No, thank you.

JANET   I won't even let Mother touch him. You should feel privileged.

SONNY   I don't go in for that kind of stuff.

JANET   Just a squeeze.

SONNY   Lay off.

JANET   Listen to him then. Put your ear there.

SONNY   What are you, nuts?

JANET   He talks.

SONNY   Keep away from me.

JANET   Listen! (SONNY *backs up as she walks toward him*) If you put your ear there, you can hear him talk. (*Follows him*) He says "MA-MA! He says "DA-DA!" Don't you want to hear the baby say "MA-MA" and "DA-DA"? (*Pause*) Go on! Listen! (*Pause*) Don't be bashful. He won't bite. (*Pause*) Would you rather see him? Is that what you want? Would you rather see the beautiful blond-haired blue-eyed baby? (*Turns around and bends over, her hands up her dress*) I'll show him to you!

SONNY   What are you doing?

JANET   Here he is! Here's the angel! Here's her little God!

> (JANET *turns back. She has a pink pillow in her hands which she has pulled out from beneath the dress. The dress now hangs limply, where before it bulged.* JANET *holds the pillow a moment for* SONNY *to see, and then suddenly tosses it at him.* SONNY, *stunned, catches it and holds it at a distance*)

Curtain

ACT TWO

It is Tuesday evening, two days later. SONNY *has taken the grandfather clock apart and is working on the mechanism.* MOTHER *comes in from kitchen carrying an iron. She watches* SONNY *work a moment.*

MOTHER   Do you really think you can fix it?

SONNY   It's a cinch.

MOTHER   I don't think it's as much in the fixing as it is in the parts. It's an heirloom . . . a family heirloom. It's been in my family for over a century. There are just no more parts available.

SONNY   It takes a little improvisation . . . that's all. Some imagination. I'm good at that. I'm handy. I'm a very handy fellow to have around.

MOTHER   It's been passed down, generation to generation . . . many of the things in this house have. There's been a certain amount of continuity in our family.

SONNY   When I'm finished with it, it'll run another hundred years. I guarantee you. I have a knack for it. I don't know the principle behind things, but I *can* take them apart and put them together. You ask me how an internal-combustion engine works and I won't be able to answer that . . . but give me a wrench and a screwdriver, and put me next to one, and I'll have it purring like a kitten.

(JANET *enters from the kitchen*)

JANET   There's coffee up. Would anyone like a cup?

SONNY   Yes . . . I think I would.

JANET   Mother?

MOTHER   No thank you, Janet. I have ironing to do. This is my first evening out in months.

(JANET *leaves. A pause*)

MOTHER   Thank you for the tickets, Sonny.

SONNY   Don't mention it!

MOTHER   I haven't been to a show in years.

FATHER (*Offstage*)   WHERE'S MY SUIT!

MOTHER (*To* SONNY)   He can never find anything.

(FATHER *appears at the head of the stairs. He is wearing a long white dress shirt which covers him to the knees, black socks and garters*)

FATHER   I can't find my suit.

MOTHER   It's in your closet.

FATHER   I looked there.

MOTHER   That's where it is.

FATHER   I just looked, I tell you. It's not there.

MOTHER   It has to be there.

FATHER   Someone stole it. It's not there. We have a thief in the house . . . a goddamn thief!

MOTHER   It's there. Look again. I know it's somewhere in the closet. (*He leaves*) I never saw anything like it. He can never find anything. He thinks people are stealing from him. He never used to be like that. He has a deathly fear of burglers. We used to leave the door open day and night. Now he checks every window and under every bed like an old maid.

FATHER (*Offstage*)   WHERE THE HELL IS IT!

MOTHER   Don't mind him though. He's just a gruff old man. (*Pause*) It's all an act though. Father acts gruff with everyone . . . but inside, he's soft as butter. He doesn't show it like I do. Not in the daytime, anyway. Only at night. He's waked up screaming every night since Ronald died. I have to give him a good rubdown before he'll fall back to sleep. (*Loud noise from upstairs*) He must have that room upside down. (*She goes up.* SONNY *continues his work.* JANET *comes in with coffee tray*)

JANET Sugar?

SONNY What?

JANET Do you want sugar?

SONNY Cubes or loose?

JANET Loose.

SONNY No sugar. I like it strong. (SONNY *sits on the couch with his cup.* JANET *starts to leave*) Aren't you having a cup?

JANET No.

SONNY Keep me company then.

JANET I have to finish the dishes.

SONNY Do you mind spending the evening with me?

JANET No. Why should I?

SONNY We'll have a good time. (*Pause*) It must be quite a while since you had a good time. (*Pause*) I promise you we'll have a good time.

JANET I have to finish the dishes.

> (JANET *leaves.* SONNY *drinks his coffee.* FATHER *comes down. He wears his pants, shirt, suspenders and shoes, and carries a suit jacket. An unmade tie is around his shoulders.* FATHER *goes to the liquor cabinet*)

48

FATHER I could use a shot. (*Takes out a bottle and shot glass*) How about you?

SONNY No thank you.

FATHER (*Pours a shot*) Where's Janet?

SONNY In the kitchen.

FATHER You don't smoke and you don't drink. What do you do? (*Downs it*) Mind you, I'm not criticizing. It's laudable. I think it's laudable. We haven't had a good, upstanding young man in this house in some time. (*Pours another shot*) Not since Ronald left, anyhow. Ronald minded all his *p*s and *q*s too. (*Downs it*) I miss him though . . . he was my son and I miss him. (*Pause*) So you're up and about now?

SONNY Yes. I was downtown yesterday. I took a walk.

FATHER You're feeling better?

SONNY Yes.

FATHER I thought so. You look better.

SONNY I feel better.

FATHER You gave us a scare Sunday. I mean, when you collapsed like that my heart skipped a beat.

SONNY I'm better now.

FATHER Good. (*Pause*) Janet told you, didn't she? She let you in on the facts?

SONNY She explained the situation.

FATHER I wasn't too rough with you, was I?

SONNY No.

FATHER Sometimes I don't know my own strength. I have to be reminded. When I was younger . . . when I was in the army, we use to wrestle around, play around, you know, wrestle about . . . a headlock, a body jab, a toe hold. You know the sport. Wrestling! I had to be reminded though. Many a time a broken bone would result from that sport. (*Goes to* SONNY *and puts his two hands out*) It's amazing, the strength in these hands! (*They look at one another for a moment.* FATHER *keeps his hands outstretched. He breaks the silence by pulling the tie from his shoulder, snapping it out straight and placing it around his neck. He ties the knot fast, one loop, watching* SONNY *while he works. He goes to the mirror and pulls it tight. The two ends are extremely uneven*) I can never get the goddamn ends even. This is why I never wear them. I have no need for the damn things anyway! (*He pulls it off. He gets bottle and glass and sits on the rocker*) I'm retired, you know. I spend my time on the ballfield or at the Democratic Club. We pass the bottle down there. We talk of the old days. When I was young I was in the center of things. I was in the army. I was in two wars and ran a business on the side. Hardware! That's what I was in! The hardware business! It would have been Ronald's, it would have been his even though he never knew a hammer from a monkey wrench. But he's dead . . . Ronald's dead now and I'm retired. (*He drinks*) Christ, he was something. You'd never believe it. You'd have to see it to believe it. He was only five, mind you. He was just a little tot. We were on the beach . . . every weekend . . . on the beach, on the sand, the hard sand . . . on the beach, near the sea. I threw him the ball, on the weekends, I threw him groundballs, flyballs, every weekend. He was a sight, his little hands, his little feet, running across the sand, grabbing the ball, catching the ball. We drew a crowd! They came out of the ocean! They came to shore to see him! That's some kid you have, mister. He's going to be a pro, they said. I was proud! I tell you, I had a father's pride! You're not a father, you wouldn't understand. (*Pause*) You have a family?

SONNY   No.

FATHER   Where you from, anyway?

SONNY   North.

FATHER   North?

SONNY   Yes.

FATHER   North where?

SONNY   Up North.

FATHER   Up North? What does that mean? What does up north mean?

SONNY   It's an expression. *Up North!* Other people say, *Down South.* I'm from *Down South,* they say. I can't say that though. I'm from *Up North!*

FATHER   I never said one or the other. I never said *Down South* or *Up North.* I'm from around here! Understand? I grew up around here! (*Pause*) This is my territory!

SONNY   I grew up in the army. That's where I came into my own. There were men there who couldn't adapt to army life, they couldn't even eat the food . . . not me, I loved the food, I had extra helpings of the food. I went through the chow line three times every morning . . . bacon, eggs sunny-side up, potatoes, milk . . . I ate my fill! They complained the food was half cooked, they wanted their bacon crisp . . . I didn't mind it half cooked, I didn't mind it at all. I filled out in the army. I matured! I became a soldier! Before that, before I was a soldier, my chest was as bare as a baby's backside. Now look! (*Pulls his shirt up, suddenly, exposing his chest. He holds the shirt up over his face*) I'm a hairy son-of-a-gun, aren't I?

   (*A long pause*)

FATHER   You know something?

SONNY   (*Behind the shirt*)   What?

FATHER   You look in the pink of health to me. I mean, you're positively glowing.

SONNY (*Tucks the shirt back into his pants*)   I feel good.

FATHER   I'm certainly glad to hear it. That takes quite a load off my mind. There's a game Sunday, you know.

SONNY   A game?

FATHER   Yes. A ballgame. This Sunday.

SONNY   That's nice.

FATHER   I want you fit. I want you fit as a fiddle. (*Pause*) I used to take Ronald out. I took him out once or twice. That was enough. Once or twice was enough. He made a fool of himself. He made a spectacle of me. Butterfingers, they called him. Butterfingers! He dropped every ball . . . he missed every chance. My son! Butterfingers! I pitched to him. I was the pitcher, you know. I lobbed the ball in. It didn't help. Nothing helped. I tell you I was disgraced. He disgraced me! It was the worst day of my life! (*He drinks*) Ronald was close to his mother. That's why she took it as bad as she did. I mean that's why she almost went batty. They had a mother-and-son relationship. He got the first slice of meat! Whenever there was a roast Ronald got the first slice . . . the outside slice . . . you know which slice I'm referring to? . . . the slice with the garlic . . . the slice with all that seasoning. He was so sweet. I tell you I would pinch him. I would pinch his little cheek. He was so sweet, butter wouldn't melt in his mouth. (*Pause*) So you're a soldier? (*Pause*) Kill many Krauts?

SONNY   Krauts?

FATHER   That's right. Krauts! Kill any?

SONNY   I can't say I have.

FATHER   You never killed a Kraut?

SONNY   No.

FATHER   What the hell kind of soldier are you?

SONNY   I think you have your wars a little confused.

FATHER   I have, have I?

SONNY   Yes, just a little. I think you have the wrong war in mind.

FATHER   I don't have the wrong war in mind, buster! Don't tell me what war I have in mind.

SONNY   Well, you see we're not fighting the Krauts any more. That was some time ago. That was another era.

   (A pause)

FATHER   Who are you fighting?

SONNY   The Chinks.

FATHER   The Chinks?

SONNY   Yes.

FATHER   You call that war? You call fighting the Chinks war? Christ, you don't know what war is all about. I could have fought the Chinks. They gave me my choice. I was an old pro, you know. I fought in the first one, so they gave me my choice in the second. I could have been stationed in the Pacific, but I chose differently. I chose the European Theater! Talk to me about war— I fought the Krauts in two World Wars. War isn't war if you're not killing Krauts. I tell you I was overjoyed to enlist in the Second World War. It was in my blood. I waited from nineteen hundred and eighteen until nineteen hundred and forty-two for that opportunity. That's a long span of years. That's twenty-four years between Krauts. When I lifted my rifle and sighted my first Kraut in twenty-four years, my life took on a different meaning. A whole new world opened up to me when I squeezed that trigger. I suddenly understood what life was all about. Those moments in life, those revelations are few and far between. (*Pause*) Stand up!

SONNY   What?

FATHER   Stand up! Go on! (*He stands*) Turn around! (*He turns a full circle*) Now walk across the room! (SONNY *walks past the stairs toward the door and stops*) You know what I think? I think you're fully recovered! I think you're entitled to a clean bill of health! (*They both stand, silently, watching one another from opposite ends of the room*) I made arrangements for Sunday.

SONNY   Arrangements?

55

FATHER   Yes. I called up the right people. The proper people, you know. I made the proper arrangements.

SONNY   What kind of arrangements?

FATHER   I made arrangements for you to play this Sunday.

SONNY   I don't know if I'll be able to.

FATHER   What do you mean?

SONNY   I may not be up to it.

FATHER   You'll be up to it. Why shouldn't you be up to it? I mean this is your prime! You're in the prime of life!

SONNY   I'm still weak in the knees.

FATHER   I gave my word! Arrangements have already been made. I can't go back on my word. My word's as good as gold! (*Pause*) They'll be waiting for you . . . all of them . . . in the field . . . in the grass . . . in the low grass . . . in the sun. They'll be waiting . . . with their bats, their balls and their gloves. You can't let them down. I gave them my word. (*Pause*) You'll be there. You'll play. I'll see to it that you play. You have to play! I made arrangements! (*Pause.* FATHER *calls* JANET) JANET! (FATHER *walks briskly to his chair and picks up his tie, snapping it tautly around his neck.* SONNY *remains where he is at the far end of the room.* JANET *enters from the kitchen.* FATHER *speaks to her as she walks in, not seeing her but sensing her presence.*

His eyes are on SONNY) Fix my tie, will you, Janet? I can't make a proper knot.

(*She goes to him and begins working on the tie*)

JANET   Have you been drinking? (*Pause*) There's coffee up. Black coffee.

FATHER   None for me. I'm on the hard stuff tonight.

(JANET *works on the tie.* FATHER *begins humming* "When the red, red robin . . ." *His body bounces. His feet move*)

JANET   I can't fix the tie if you're going to move.

FATHER   I always move when I hum! I can't help myself! My feet get going!

JANET   Don't hum then!

FATHER   (*Hums and then stops*) See this girl. I owe her everything. I owe her the world. If it wasn't for her, Mother would be in the bobby hatch.

JANET   Be quiet, Father.

FATHER   Credit where credit is due. Janet is the only thing standing between mother and the booby hatch.

JANET   *Shhh!*

FATHER   (*Hugs her*) I love this girl!

57

JANET   Stop it, Father!

FATHER   (*Continues*) I love her as if she was my own flesh and blood.

JANET   You're embarrassing me!

FATHER   The only good thing Ronald ever did was marry her.

> (*He continues hugging her.* MOTHER *appears at the head of the stairs in a green dress. She stands and watches them.* SONNY, *standing by the stairs, is the only one to see her*)

MOTHER (*To* SONNY)   Do you like this dress?

SONNY   You'll take their breath away!

> (FATHER *stops hugging* JANET. *They stand apart*)

FATHER (*Apologetically*)   Janet's making me a knot.

MOTHER (*Ignores him, speaking to* SONNY)   This was Ronald's favorite. I wore it when he was a child. Every Sunday he would ask me to wear it. He would ask me to wear my green dress. (MOTHER *walks down the stairs* toward JANET *and* FATHER) Do you remember, Father, how we would dress up on Sundays? We went out every Sunday! Ronald would walk between us and hold our hands and every so often we would swing him up and fly him in the air. Do you remember how he laughed? How the three of us laughed? What good times we had then!

(*Pause*) I think it's an omen, Sonny's coming. I think it's an omen of good luck. Don't you agree? I think it means that everything will be fine from now on. That Janet's baby will be born healthy. (*Pause. She goes to* JANET, *who backs up a step*) I'm not ashamed to pray for that. (*She gets on her knees before* JANET) I'm not ashamed to get on my hands and knees and pray that the baby will be well. I'm not ashamed to pray to God he'll be like Ronald . . . look like Ronald . . . speak like Ronald. I'm not ashamed to pray to God.

Blackout

SCENE 2

It is half an hour later. SONNY, *alone in the living room, is sitting on* FATHER's *rocker, drinking.* SONNY *goes to liquor cabinet with the empty glass. The cabinet is open, with bottles all about. He picks up one bottle at a time, examining them closely, finds what he wants and pours himself a drink. He walks to the stairs with the glass and listens. He drinks. He wanders about the room, stops at* MOTHER's *chair, puts the glass down and picks up her Bible. There is a ribbon-marker in it. He turns to the page and reads a passage aloud.*

"Now when Jesus was born in Bethlehem of Judea in the days of Herod the King, behold, there came Wise Men from the East to Jerusalem, saying, Where is He that is born King of the Jews? For we have seen His star in the East, and are come to worship Him."

JANET *appears at the top of the stairs. She is not wearing the pillow. She is wearing a topcoat, fully buttoned, and high heels. She is carrying a suitcase. She watches* SONNY. *He turns and sees her.*

SONNY   Janet! (*Long pause*) You startled me. (JANET *starts down the stairs with the suitcase*)

JANET   I'm leaving!

SONNY   Leaving?

JANET   This is my opportunity. They've never been away for an evening. They never go out.

SONNY   What happens when they come back?

JANET   I won't be here!

SONNY   Is there anything you want me to tell her, any particular message you want me to convey?

JANET   I want to get out of here. Don't you understand?

SONNY   What's the rush? You have all evening. They won't be back until late tonight.

JANET   This is not the first time I've packed. I've packed and unpacked a dozen times in the last six months. I was packed only last week, right before you came. I was ready to sneak out, in the middle of the night. I couldn't go through with it though. I didn't have the nerve. I've never had the nerve. I felt sorry for her.

SONNY   Sit down. Let's talk about it.

JANET   There's nothing to talk about. It won't be so bad for Mother. You're here now. You can take my place.

SONNY   I'm not pregnant.

JANET   Neither am I!

SONNY   She doesn't know that though. She thinks you
are.

JANET   That's not my fault. That was Father's idea. He
sweet-talked me. I was pregnant six months ago. I was
nine months pregnant. We were in the living room. It
was the evening of the second day after the news of
Ronald's death. We were in mourning. I was nine
months pregnant and in mourning. Mother was in her
chair. Father in his rocker. It was warm that night.
Stuffy, really. There were people in the house. Strange
faces. They had been coming all afternoon and by evening the house was finally filled. There was food on the
table. Wine. Liquor. Everyone was eating. Everyone
was drinking. People were speaking to me, strangers,
whispering in my ear . . . offering condolences. I could
hardly breathe. It was stifling. There was no oxygen in
the room. Those strangers were consuming all the
oxygen. Someone was wiping my face, patting it with
a damp cloth. Someone gave me water and somebody
else . . . food. Keep up your strength, Dearie, they
whispered, You'll need it. It was dark out. Evening. The
door was open. People were still coming. The house
was filled, but they still came. The men wore black ties
and suits, the women, dark dresses. They were smiling
and nodding. Everyone was eating . . . drinking . . .
talking. I stood up. I felt ill. I tried to go upstairs. It
was impossible. The staircase was jammed. There was
no room to move . . . no air to breathe. Someone cried
out! I thought I heard a cry. It came from outside.

Someone was crying outside. I pushed my way to the door. The cry was louder now. It was a scream. I looked out. It was dark. I could see nothing. I turned around and ran in. I rushed back into the room. The sound was unbearable. It was closer now, louder, it was in the room. No one moved. They were silent. They were watching me. All of their eyes were on me. What's the matter with you? Don't you hear it? I yelled. Don't you hear that scream? I cupped my hands over my ears to drown out the awful sound of it . . . and then for the first time I understood why no one else but I heard it. The scream was not coming from without but from *within,* from *within* me, from deep *within* my flesh. It was my child who was screaming, my infant who was suffocating. The sound I heard was the terrible agony of its death.

(SONNY *has been sitting and listening. He offers* JANET *his drink*)

SONNY   Here. Drink this. You'll feel better.

JANET (*Drinks it*) I fainted. When I woke up I was in the hospital. The baby was dead. He was born dead. Mother went to pieces. She could accept Ronald's death, but not this, not the two deaths one after the other. It was Father's idea . . . the pillow. When Mother saw me pregnant again she calmed down. Father said it would only be for a day or two . . . until she regained her strength, until she was strong enough to accept the truth. If I listened to him I would be here forever. I would remain nine months pregnant the rest of my life.

(JANET *holds the empty glass in her hand.* SONNY *pours her another drink. She drinks it automatically.* SONNY *puts the bottle back in the cabinet*)

SONNY   It's warm in here. Let me help you off with your coat. (JANET *stands and* SONNY *helps her off with the coat. Underneath, she wears the low-cut dress*) Janet! You're wearing my dress! (*Pause*) That's the dress I bought you!

JANET   Everything else was packed.

SONNY   I'm not complaining. I'm just surprised, that's all. I never expected anything like this.

JANET   Like what?

SONNY   I mean I did expect it in the beginning. This is how Ronald described you. This is what I had in mind all along! It comes as a shock though. I've become accustomed to your big belly.

JANET   This dress was out, so I put it on.

SONNY   Come on, Janet. Don't kid me.

JANET   What do you mean?

SONNY   You know you wore that dress on purpose.

JANET   I did?

SONNY   Yes. You had no intention of leaving. You needed a little coaxing, that's all.

64

JANET   I don't know what you're talking about.

SONNY   You weren't about to walk out on me. After all, I have a lot to offer. (*Pause*) There are a number of women who like prisoners. Men who have been imprisoned. They wait by the gates. The longer the confinement the better. These women live in the towns that surround prisons. You can see them there in the bars and restaurants, smoking, waiting. They're usually thin, nervous types. They like all that energy . . . all that pent-up sex. They want it all. Isn't that what you want, Janet? Isn't that what you've been waiting for?

JANET   No!

     (*A Pause*)

SONNY   I didn't think so. Not from what Ronald said, anyway.

JANET   What did he say?

SONNY   Not much at first. You see, in the beginning there were three of us. We had order then. The major took charge. As long as the major was there everything was neat and proper. But he left us . . . there was an exchange, you see, and we were left alone . . . high and dry, so to speak. It was a nasty place, that prison . . . dark . . . hot . . . none of the comforts. There was water close by . . . we heard the sound of rushing water, but all they gave us was filth. After the major left, things deteriorated. We lived like animals. We were no longer concerned about personal hygiene. We wallowed in our own filth. Ronald became delirious. He said things I'm sure he would have retracted had he been fully conscious.

JANET   What kind of things?

SONNY   I'll never forgive the major for leaving. His duty was there with us. We needed him! We needed his authority! He left us though. I had respected him. I had respected the major. He was the only man I ever did respect . . . although it was more fear than respect. After all, he was an officer.

JANET   What did Ronald say?

SONNY   He said certain things. He implied certain things.

JANET   Why did he leave? There was no reason for him to enlist. He could have been exempt. He had a history of poor health. (*Pause*) He was so quiet. I never knew what was on his mind. One day he was sitting, staring into space. I asked him what he was thinking about. He said he was thinking of me, that's what he had been thinking of . . . me.

(*A pause*)

SONNY   Why don't you remove your dress?

JANET   What?

SONNY   Take your dress off.

(*A pause*)

JANET   You must be crazy.

SONNY   Not at all. It'll just be much simpler if you remove your dress.

(*Janet stands up*)

JANET   Let me have my coat.

SONNY   What for?

JANET   I'm leaving.

SONNY   We've been through that already.

JANET   Give me my coat!

SONNY   Come and get it!

(*He holds it out to her. She reaches for it. He pulls
it back. She reaches again. He pulls it back again.
She moves closer. He holds it behind him. She
tries to get it.* SONNY *laughs*)

JANET   I'll leave without it! (*She goes to her suitcase,
picks it up and starts for the door.* SONNY *rushes to the
door ahead of her*) Get out of my way!

SONNY   You're not going anywhere. Not right now, at
any rate. We have some unfinished business to settle.

JANET   What are you talking about!

(SONNY *reaches out and touches her breast. She moves back*)

SONNY Don't be shy. There's nothing to be shy about. You should consider me an old friend. (*He walks toward her. She backs away*) Ronald told me all about you. I know what gets you going. I know what button to push.

JANET What did he tell you about me?

SONNY Everything! Ronald told me everything. He drove me crazy! He told me the most intimate details. (JANET *drops her suitcase and backs off into the room.* SONNY *follows*) It was as if you were alive there in that hut. I could actually feel you! I could smell you! I could even taste you, Janet! You were on the very tip of my tongue! "Do you mind?" I asked Ronald. "Do you mind? After all, she is your wife." "It's my pleasure," he said. "Go ahead! Enjoy her! Enjoy the bitch! She needs a good screwing!" So I took you, Janet . . . I took you there in that dark prison with Ronald beside me, goading me on. (*Pause*) The things you did there, Janet. My God! It shocked Ronald! It even surprised me. There was no limit to your perversion. We both used you, one at a time, and sometimes together. (*Pause*) So you see, there's no reason to be modest. I've already been over the terrain.

(JANET *runs for the door without her suitcase.* SONNY *follows and grabs her from behind. She struggles to get away*)

JANET Leave go of me!

68

SONNY Where do you think you're going? You're staying right here! (*She struggles. He slaps her back and forth across the face. She falls to the floor*) This is how Ronald should have handled you. It would have kept you in your place. You want to be kept in your place, don't you, Janet? You like being slapped around? Isn't that right? (*She tries to get up. He pushes her down with his shoe*) It's too bad Ronald's not here. I could have given him lessons! (JANET *lies on the floor.* SONNY *stands near her, legs spread*) You're going to do it every whichway with me, Janet. *I'm* not Ronald! There are a number of variations I have in mind. (JANET *crawls toward him*) It looks to me like you're ready. Am I right, Janet? *Are* you ready? (*She encircles his feet with her arms and looks up at him*) I do believe you are! I do believe you're ready!

Blackout

It is Sunday, noon. The church bells are ringing. The grandfather clock is working.

A table upstage is opened. There is food out . . . a colorful display of jams, fruit, cakes, cookies, etc.

MOTHER *enters from kitchen with a large bowl of jam. She places it on the table and then walks around, arranging everything.*

MOTHER (*calls*) We need some more silver, Janet. There aren't enough serving spoons. (*Pause*) And a carving knife: Don't forget the carving knife! (*Picks up a large knife and tests it on her palm. She speaks to herself*) This knife will never do. It hasn't been sharpened in years. (MOTHER *exits into kitchen with knife.* JANET *enters from kitchen with serving spoons and carving knife. She looks different. Effervescent! She wears her hair down. She places each serving spoon into a bowl of jam, then places the carving knife next to a large round loaf of bread.* MOTHER *enters with another bowl of jam*) This will be a nice surprise. They'll be like a couple of hungry wolves when they come back from the game. They'll be able to dig right in. (*Pause*) How does it look, Janet? Does it look nice?

JANET Lovely.

MOTHER It does look appetizing. (*Pause.* JANET *is at the table*) I don't know whatever made you change the style of your hair.

JANET I didn't change it. I'm just wearing it down.

MOTHER It's too hot to wear down. Besides, you're pregnant! It's much more comfortable up.

JANET I like it down.

MOTHER This summer has been terrible. The summers have been getting hotter and the winters colder. I don't like to go out any more. There's no shade on this street. The trees are bare. We had a tree surgeon here a few years ago. He said they were diseased. At that time there were only two or three trees that were leafless; now the whole block is that way. A disease like that spreads like the plague. God knows what's happening on the other blocks. The whole neighborhood may be in the sun! (JANET *breaks open a small roll and spreads jam on it*) I can't get over the change in you these past few days, Janet. Why, you even have your appetite back. (JANET *sits on the couch and eats the roll and jam*) I think that's a good sign . . . the fact that your appetite is improving. (MOTHER *goes to the window and looks out*) They should be home soon. I wonder how the game went. I hope Sonny was up to it.

JANET I'm sure he was.

MOTHER   He's only been here a week. I don't think he's rested sufficiently.

JANET   Sonny can take care of himself.

MOTHER   That game can get out of hand, you know. Father's come home many a Sunday with a bruise. I heard him say this morning, before they left, that that's where they separate the men from the boys . . . on that ballfield. (*Pause*) I don't know how that man does it . . . every Sunday . . . every single Sunday. Where does he find the energy? (*Pause*) When it comes time for bed, he's just the opposite. He's just like a baby. He'll whimper and complain, and I'll have to rub him down and soothe him and put him to bed. (*Pause*) Is the coffee up, Janet?

JANET   No.

MOTHER   They'll be home soon. I better make it. They'll want it nice and strong.

> (MOTHER *goes into the kitchen.* JANET *sits on the couch.* SONNY *comes in. He wears his customary outfit, boots, khakis. He is dirtied and disheveled*)

SONNY   Hello.

JANET   Hello.

SONNY   Where's Mother?

JANET   In the kitchen. (*Pause*) Where's Father?

SONNY   He'll be along soon. I got a head start.

(JANET *gets up and goes to him. They stand apart*)

JANET   I've been waiting for you.

SONNY   You have?

JANET   Yes. All morning.

SONNY   I was with you the whole night. Can't you do without me one morning?

JANET   No.

SONNY   Got the hots, huh?

JANET   I've been thinking about you. I get wet just thinking about you.

SONNY   Can't get enough, can you?

JANET   No. I can't get enough.

SONNY   Well, we'll have to do something about that.

JANET   Yes, we will. (SONNY *goes to the table and walks around it, looking at the food*) Let's go upstairs.

SONNY   Now?

JANET   Yes.

SONNY   In broad daylight?

JANET   We'll close the shades.

SONNY   I appreciate your enthusiasm, Janet, but I don't think this is the proper moment. I mean, there's a time and place for everything.

JANET   What's wrong with right now?

SONNY   Nothing. Except Father will be home any moment and Mother will wonder where we are.

JANET   I don't care.

SONNY   I do! After all, I'm just a guest. You're not! You're a member of the household! You can come and go as you please. (*Pause*) I don't think it would be proper. I mean, look at the table Mother has set! I don't think it would be in the best of taste for us to go upstairs and fuck. (*Pause*) This is very artistically arranged. Very tempting. You don't mind that I have a bite right now, do you? I worked up quite an appetite on the ballfield. What is this . . . strawberry preserve? (*Tastes it with his finger*) Mmmmm! Delicious! (*Cuts a slice of bread*) There's nothing like a freshly sliced piece of bread covered with strawberry preserve. Would you like some, Janet? Want me to cut you a slice?

JANET   I just had a slice.

SONNY   One slice! Don't be silly. Let me fix you up another. You have to keep up your strength. Strawberry preserve is better than oysters. You're going to need your strength, Janet. You have to keep in shape for our little bouts.

(*He cuts her a slice and spreads the jam.* MOTHER *comes in*)

MOTHER Sonny! When did you come in?

SONNY Just now.

MOTHER I didn't hear you. (*Watches him spread the jam*) That's right, Sonny. Help yourself. I have coffee brewing in the kitchen. Strong coffee.

SONNY That sounds wonderful.

MOTHER Don't forget the apricot and apple preserve.

SONNY I won't. I'm sampling the strawberry right now.

MOTHER Where's Father?

SONNY He's coming. This is just delicious, Mother. This is some spread.

MOTHER Why aren't you together?

(*A pause*)

SONNY There was an accident.

MOTHER An accident?

SONNY   Yes. It was unfortunate . . . but that's one of the hazards of the game.

MOTHER   Is Father all right?

SONNY   There was some damage to his hand. And maybe his shoulder. I'm not sure about the shoulder, but I am sure about the hand.

MOTHER   Ohhh. God!

SONNY   It was unavoidable. A hard-hit ball, you understand. (*There is a loud bellow outside. They stand and listen a moment*) I tried to help him. He wouldn't let me. His teammates are bringing him home.

(MOTHER *rushes to the window and looks out*)

MOTHER   They're supporting him. They're half carrying him.

FATHER   (*From outside*) LEAVE GO OF ME, YOU BASTARDS! I'M NOT AN INVALID YET! (*The door flies open.* FATHER *appears. His shoulder seems lopsided and he is holding his pitching hand to his body*) There he is! There's the bastard that did it!

MOTHER   Oh, my God!

FATHER   (*Walks unsteadily to his rocker*) There's the bastard that broke my hand!

SONNY   It was an accident.

FATHER (*Sitting*) An accident my eye! It was deliberate! He deliberately set out to maim me! (*His glove comes flying through the open door, followed by each of his spiked shoes*) Close the goddamn door! Keep those bastards out of here!

(JANET *closes the door*)

MOTHER (*To* FATHER) Let me see it.

(*She touches it lightly.* FATHER *bellows in pain*)

FATHER Jesus Christ! Keep your hands off of me. Get me some ice! Ice is what I need!

JANET I'll get it!

(JANET *goes into the kitchen*)

MOTHER I'll call a doctor.

FATHER No, no doctor!

MOTHER If it's broken you need a doctor.

FATHER I don't need a doctor. I'll doctor it myself.

MOTHER It has to be set if it's broken. It has to be put in a cast.

FATHER I've done without a doctor for sixty-seven years, I'm not starting now. (*Holds his hand up*) Christ! Look at it! (*Pause*) Where's the ice? What the hell is holding up the ice?

MOTHER (*Calls*) Janet!

JANET (*From the kitchen*) Coming!

MOTHER It has to be set. It looks broken to me.

FATHER That's the bastard. Standing over there. Sonny-boy! He ruined me.

SONNY It was an accident.

FATHER He hit the ball right at me. A line drive. I had no time to react. I was off stride! It hit my bare hand . . . my pitching hand.

SONNY I can't control where the ball goes. I just swing at it. I swing with all my might.

(JANET *comes in with a bowl of ice*)

JANET Here!

(*She sets it down in front of* FATHER. *He looks at it for a moment*)

FATHER Am I supposed to dip my bare hand into a bucket of ice? I need a towel! For Christ sake someone get me a towel! (MOTHER *runs into the kitchen for one*) I'm surrounded by incompetence!

(JANET *walks over and picks up one of the spiked shoes. She puts it down, walking seductively past* SONNY. *She walks back toward the door and picks up another shoe. While she is bent over she turns to see if* SONNY *is watching. She brings that shoe*

*back also, and then returns for the glove. She re-
mains bent over, provocatively, her backside in the
air; she wiggles it.* SONNY *walks slowly to her.*
MOTHER *has come back with a towel and is putting
ice in it.* FATHER, *seated facing them, sees what is
happening.* SONNY *walks behind her, reaches down
and cups her breasts, pulling her up. Her back is
toward him*)

SONNY (*Holding her*) Why don't you go upstairs and
wait for me, Janet. I'll be up in a minute or two. Go up
and get yourself ready. You know what I mean.

(JANET *puts the glove down and goes up.* FATHER
smolders in his seat. MOTHER *takes his hand and
wraps the towel around it.* FATHER *bellows*)

FATHER Don't touch me! I'll do it myself! (FATHER *takes
the towel and circles it about his hand*) Stay away! If
you want to help, get me some water. I'm parched! My
insides are parched!

(MOTHER *hurries into the kitchen.* SONNY, *near the
food table, watches* FATHER)

SONNY Have you noticed the snack the little ladies pre-
pared for us, Father? It's a shame to let it go to waste.
Can I fix you something? Some jam perhaps? (*Pause*)
If you don't want anything, do you mind if I nibble a bit?
(*Cuts himself a slice*) I think I'll try the apricot this time.

(MOTHER *comes into the room with a glass of water.
She holds it up to* FATHER'*s mouth. He swallows a
mouthful and then spits it out on the rug, coughing
violently*)

FATHER   That's sink water!

MOTHER   We're out of spring water.

FATHER   You gave me a glass of sink water!

MOTHER   The jug is empty. What should I do?

FATHER   Nothing! Let me die in peace!

MOTHER   I'll call a doctor.

FATHER   I'm going up. I'm going up to bed. (*He stands up cautiously and walks toward the stairs. He stops in the middle of the room, his body contorted*) It's my shoulder. My shoulder is out of joint.

MOTHER   I'm not waiting any longer. I'm calling the doctor.

> (MOTHER *leaves for the kitchen.* FATHER *stands contorted in the middle of the room.* SONNY *stands at the table, eating*)

SONNY   If you like I'll give you a helping hand.

FATHER   Stay your distance!

SONNY   I know exactly what you need. If you let me, I'll manipulate your shoulder back into place.

FATHER   Stay away from me. I'm wise to you.

SONNY   What's the matter? Can't take a little pain?

FATHER   I can take pain, all right!

SONNY   I don't think you can. I think you're a big blow-hard. You're afraid to let me touch you.

FATHER   Go ahead then! Touch me! (SONNY *walks over to him*) I can take anything you dish out! Anything! (SONNY *stands behind* FATHER, *placing his hands on his shoulders and pressing down.* FATHER *bellows*) Go ahead! This is child's play. I've had my share of pain. I've suffered plenty in my time. Years ago there was a drought in this area. A major drought! The stream dried up. I was only a boy at the time but I was on my own. I hid in the forest. I was thirsty but I couldn't go near the stream. The animals were fighting. They were ripping each other to pieces. I had to hide out for days. It was a massacre. A bloody massacre! I crawled past their carcasses. The stream was red. It was thick with their guts. I drank . . . and then I vomited. I drank again, and threw up again. I had no other choice. I had to drink! I had to live! There were other men around the stream, drinking . . . and birds, huge birds with beaks, vultures! The men had come out of the forest. They had kept their wits about them. They waited till the fighting was over. Then they drank their fill. We quenched our thirst at that bloody stream. But not our hunger! We craved meat! We tore into those bloody carcasses. We clawed our way through their open wounds. We chewed them to the bone! It was a feasting ground. We gorged ourselves! I was in pain for days. I tossed and turned in pain on that bloody ground for days. (FATHER *bellows again.* SONNY *has been pressing him slowly down until he has finally fallen to his knees*) You tell me I can't take

pain! I can take pain! I can take all the pain in the world!
Go on! Give it to me! Give me all you got!

(FATHER *is on his knees,* SONNY *over him, pressing
his shoulders.* FATHER *bellows one last time as the
act ends*)

Curtain

ACT THREE

It is one month later, afternoon.

MOTHER, *alone in the living room, reads the Bible.*

SONNY *enters from the kitchen, carrying an empty water jug. He stops and watches* MOTHER *read. There is a long silence.*

SONNY   Do you prefer the Old or the New?

MOTHER   I beg your pardon?

SONNY   I notice you've been reading the Gospels. Do you prefer them over the Old Testament?

MOTHER   I don't care for the Old Testament at all. I never have . . . even as a child. There's too much obscenity in it . . . too much violence and perversion. It's just too bloody for my taste.

SONNY   Yes, it is that—it is bloody.

MOTHER   The New Testament is about our gentle Lord and Saviour.

SONNY   As I recall . . . He came to a bloody end Himself, crucified as He was, nailed to the cross as He was. I wouldn't call that pleasant reading.

MOTHER I never read that far. I never read about the Crucifixion itself. (SONNY *walks to the door*) Are you going now?

SONNY Yes. I'll just fill up the jug. I won't be gone long.

MOTHER It's hot out today.

SONNY Yes, I know.

MOTHER Aren't you warm in those boots?

SONNY I don't mind.

MOTHER Would you do me a favor before you go, Sonny?

SONNY What is it?

MOTHER Come here. (SONNY *walks over to* MOTHER. *He stands there a moment. She gets up, goes behind her chair, bends over out of sight and then stands, holding out a pair of shoes*) Try on these.

SONNY What are they?

MOTHER Shoes. Loafers really. Ronald's loafers. They're much more appropriate for this weather.

SONNY I prefer my boots, thank you.

MOTHER Try them on anyway. See if they fit you.

SONNY I don't wear loafers.

MOTHER They should fit. You have the same build as Ronald. (*Pause*) Go on, Sonny. Try them on just for size. You don't have to wear them. (*She forces them on him.* SONNY *sits and takes his boots off*) I don't know why I never thought of this before. Ronald's closet is filled with clothes. There's any number of things you could wear. Everything of his is there . . . everything except his pictures.

SONNY (*Putting on the loafers*) Where are they?

MOTHER This is the only one left . . . this baby picture I carry in my locket. He went through the family album the night before he left and cut himself out of every picture. Even his wedding photographs. He took a scissors and clipped himself out. The only evidence of his existence is an occasional hand or arm around one of our shoulders. (SONNY *stands up*) How are they?

SONNY Fine.

MOTHER They fit?

SONNY Perfectly.

(MOTHER *picks his boots up and holds them*)

MOTHER You won't have to break them in, either. They're already broken in.

SONNY I prefer my boots, really.

MOTHER Walk on them. See how they feel.

87

SONNY   They feel fine! I told you that.

MOTHER   You can always change when you come home. Wear them for a while! (*Pause.* SONNY *picks the jug up*) These are too warm for this time of year. You'll see! You'll feel much better in loafers! (SONNY *leaves.* MOTHER *puts the boots down. She sits in her chair, opens her locket and stares at the photo*) He was such a lovely little boy. He looked just like an angel, with his blond hair and his blue eyes. (FATHER *appears at the head of the stairs. He has a cast on his hand*) Later his hair got darker, and his eyes too.

FATHER   I'm hungry!

MOTHER   (*Closes her locket*)   Dinner won't be ready for another two hours.

FATHER   I'm hungry now!

MOTHER   If you eat now you'll spoil your appetite.

> (MOTHER *knits.* FATHER *walks down the stairs. He walks to the door*)

FATHER   This door is open! It's unlatched! (*Pause*) Do you hear me? I said someone left this door open!

MOTHER   Close it then! Close it and lock it.

FATHER   (*Locks it*)   Whenever I leave the room someone unlatches the door. I lock the door ten times a day. (*Pause*) I have a suspicion who it could be. I have a

good suspicion. I'll catch him in the act one day . . .
wait and see . . . I'll set a trap and catch him in the act.

MOTHER   Your laces are untied.

FATHER   What?

MOTHER   If I were you I would be concerned with my
shoelaces, not with the door.

FATHER   You're not me!

MOTHER   If you trip on your laces you can fall and break
your other hand.

FATHER   Don't worry about my laces.

MOTHER   Why won't you wear your bedroom slippers?

FATHER   I'm dressed, that's why! I'm wearing my shirt
and pants. When I'm in my bathrobe and pajamas I'll
wear my bedroom slippers, when I'm dressed I'll wear
my shoes.

MOTHER   There's no difference.

FATHER   There's no difference between dayclothes and
nightclothes?

MOTHER   Slippers can be worn at any time.

FATHER   Don't you think I would tie my laces if I could?

I would like nothing better than to be able to tie my laces. Who the hell wants to walk around all day with their laces dragging behind?

MOTHER   That's easily remedied.

FATHER   Do you have any idea of the hours I spent the last month trying to tie my laces with my one hand? It would astound you! The hours spent would astound you! It can't be done. I've devoted whole days to that problem. It just can't be done!

MOTHER   I would be happy to tie them for you. It would save you all that time and work.

FATHER   You'll see me dead first!

MOTHER   Father!

FATHER   That's right! You'll see me dead in my coffin before you'll tie my laces. After they've embalmed me . . . after they've stretched me out and taken my blood and sewed my lips together . . . then you can tie my laces!

MOTHER   You'll be as good as new after the cast is off.

FATHER   I'll never be as good as new.

MOTHER   That's what the doctor said.

FATHER   This is my pitching hand.

MOTHER   It's not such a tragedy. You were getting too old for it anyway.

FATHER   I was getting too old?

MOTHER   Yes. Your pitching days would have had to come to an end sooner or later.

FATHER   A good twenty years! (*Pause*) There are exceptions, you know. Exceptional men. Men who can perform their jobs until the very day they die. Williams could have gone on hitting. He never lost his timing. Cobb too . . . and DiMaggio. It got them in the legs . . . that's the first thing to go, the legs, but my legs are as strong as iron and so was my arm. I could have pitched till the day I died.

MOTHER   You can enjoy your retirement now. You can sit in your rocker and relax like the other men your age.

FATHER (*Under his breath*)   Jesus.

(JANET *comes down. She has a hairbrush. She goes to a mirror in the living room and brushes her hair, languorously*)

MOTHER   What you need is a hobby . . . an outside interest. Something that's not strenuous. (*Pause*) Gardening, for example.

FATHER (*Sits in the rocker, speaks softly*)   Jesus God.

MOTHER   If you don't fancy cultivating a garden, you can

always take care of the weeds on the lawn. You can spend your afternoons pulling up the weeds. (FATHER *closes his eyes and rocks. Pause.*) Have you noticed the change in Janet, Father?

FATHER (*Stops rocking*)   Change? (*Pause*) What change?

MOTHER   You haven't noticed?

FATHER   I don't know what change you're referring to!

MOTHER   I'm surprised you haven't noticed. Her whole personality seems to have undergone a change. Janet is a different person!

FATHER   Now that you mention it . . . I have noticed a change!

(JANET *goes to the window and looks out. She continues brushing her hair*)

JANET   I think Sonny did a wonderful job on the house.

MOTHER   He only used one coat of paint! It's the way you apply it, he told me. If you know what you're doing, one coat can be as good as two or three.

JANET   I could never tell it was only one coat.

MOTHER   That's the mark of a professional.

FATHER   There was nothing wrong with this house before he came.

MOTHER   It was faded. It was all washed out.

FATHER   Who cares! We're inside . . . not outside. Who cares what it looks like outside? It's inside that counts! It's in here that we do our living!

(*A pause*)

MOTHER   Do you see him, Janet?

JANET   No. (JANET *goes back to the mirror. A Pause*)

FATHER   (*Rocking*) What are we having for dinner anyway?

MOTHER   A roast.

FATHER   Roast beef?

MOTHER   That's right.

FATHER   Roast beef, huh? (*Pause*) It seems to me we had a number of roasts recently.

MOTHER   I thought you liked them.

FATHER   I do. That's not the point. I love roasts. I'll take a roast any day.

MOTHER   What is the point?

FATHER   The point is, before he came along, we were lucky to have a roast once a month. Now we have one every other day.

MOTHER   It's good red meat. Sonny needs the strength.

(*A pause*)

FATHER   Why is it that he gets the first slice?

MOTHER   You're not starting that old business?

FATHER   What old business?

MOTHER   He gets the first slice because he's the guest. After the roast has been sliced the plate is first passed to the guest.

FATHER   Why is it that the guest always takes the first slice? Answer me that! Why hasn't the guest ever left the first slice for me?

MOTHER   That's his prerogative!

FATHER   I wish I was a guest . . . just *once* . . . I wish I was a goddamn guest! (*Pause*) I'm hungry! (*Pause*) If you just cut me a tiny slice it'll tide me over till dinner.

MOTHER   The meat is raw. It's not done.

FATHER   I don't mind. I prefer it that way.

MOTHER   There's pudding.

FATHER   I don't want pudding.

MOTHER   There's chocolate pudding.

FATHER   I don't want *dessert!* I want a piece of meat. I want something I can sink my teeth into.

MOTHER   I can't cut the roast. It's out of the question! (*Pause*) I can fix you some cheese and crackers though. (*She gets up*) That should hold you over. I'll fix you a plate of cheese and crackers.

> (MOTHER *goes into the kitchen.* JANET *goes to the window again, brushing her hair.* FATHER *gets up from the rocker and sits on the couch*)

FATHER   Come here, Janet.

JANET   What do you want?

FATHER   Come and sit by me.

JANET   I'm busy.

FATHER   You're busy? (*Pause*) You're busy, you say? (*Pause*) I know what's keeping you busy. I know what's on your mind.

JANET   You do?

FATHER   I have eyes. I have ears. I know what's happening around here.

JANET   What *is* happening?

FATHER   Don't think you can pull the wool over my eyes. I'm an old hand at the game. (*Gets up and goes halfway to her, speaks quietly*) I hear you in the night. I hear the two of you. I've been up a number of nights this past month. I heard the commotion. (*Closer to her, hissing at her*) Aren't you ashamed? Aren't you ashamed of yourself?

JANET   No!

FATHER   I thought you were respectable. I thought you were a respectable person.

JANET   Sorry to disappoint you.

FATHER   It's that bastard's fault. He did this to you. He made a slut out of you.

JANET   I think you're right.

FATHER   Thank God Ronald is not alive.

JANET   Yes . . . thank God for that.

FATHER   What would he say? What would Ronald say if he could see you now?

JANET   I don't care what he would say. He's not alive. He's dead. He's dead and good riddance to him.

FATHER   What?

JANET   That's right! You heard me right. Good riddance!

FATHER   I can't believe my ears.

JANET   I was sorry I ever married him. What did I ever see in him, anyway? He was gentle, but he had no backbone. He wasn't like Sonny . . . or for that matter, even like you. He didn't even take after you! He wasn't even half the man his father was!

MOTHER (*From the kitchen*)   Come in, Father!

JANET   When the telegram came that he died, I was relieved . . . I was relieved to be rid of him.

> (*Silence.* FATHER *stares at* JANET. *He turns and walks slowly into the kitchen.* JANET *watches him leave and then turns back to the window. She sees* SONNY *and runs to the door and opens it.* SONNY *enters, carrying the heavy jug of water*)

SONNY (*Carries it to a table*)   This weighs a ton! I don't know how the old man does it. (*Puts it down*) You could bust a gut! (JANET *closes the door and watches him*) How are you today, Janet? You look chipper. (*Pause*) The streets are burning. It's as bad out there as it was in the tropics. (*Pause*) Where is everyone?

JANET   In the kitchen.

SONNY   Do you know the stream was bubbling. When I bent over to fill up the jug I actually saw the water bubble. I never saw that before. We had plenty of hot days in the tropics . . . real scorchers . . . but I never witnessed that phenomenon before.

JANET (*Comes to him*)   I'm pregnant.

SONNY   What?

JANET   I said I'm pregnant.

SONNY   Pregnant? (*Pause. He treats it as a joke*) Is that
a fact? (*He taps on her belly and laughs*) I never would
have guessed!

JANET   I mean I *am* pregnant!
(*A pause*)

SONNY   You're pregnant?

JANET   Yes.

SONNY   Son of a gun! (*Pause*) Are you sure?

JANET   Yes. I'm positive.

SONNY   How can you be so sure?

JANET   I know the signs. I've been through it once before.

SONNY   Son of a gun!

JANET   You're happy?

SONNY   Happy? I'm overjoyed!

JANET   I wasn't sure how you would take it.

SONNY   I'm overjoyed, I tell you! I'm ecstatic!

JANET   What are we going to do?

SONNY   Don't worry about that now. There's plenty of time for that later. (*Goes to the liquor cabinet*) This calls for a drink. This calls for a toast. (*Taking out bottles*) I'm a father! I'm going to be a goddamn father!

JANET   (*Puts her finger to her mouth*) Shhh!

SONNY   It's not every day someone is created in your image. (*More bottles*) What are you drinking?

JANET   Anything.

SONNY   There's bourbon . . . Scotch . . . vodka . . .

JANET   I don't care.

SONNY   You don't have a baby every day. Although *you* certainly look like *you* might have one every day. How about bourbon? This bottle hasn't been touched. I think I'll break open a bottle of Father's bourbon. (*Breaks it open*) I don't think he'll mind . . . after all, it is an occasion. (*Pours two shots*) Here! Drink up! (*He clicks her glass. They drink.* SONNY *finishes his,* JANET *only sips hers*) How about another?

JANET   No.

SONNY   I think I'll have another. After all, I'm going to be a father. (*Pours himself a shot*) I knew it was imminent, though. I'm highly potent, you see. I knew once

99

we got started, it was just a matter of time. (*He drinks*)
It's bound to be a boy. There's no doubt about it in my
mind. (*Pause*) You can call him Ronald!

(*A pause*)

JANET That's not funny.

SONNY It wasn't meant to be funny. I think Ronald is a
damn good name for a boy. I would be proud to have
a son of mine named Ronald. (FATHER *enters holding
a plate of cheese and crackers*) Father! You're just in
time to join us in a toast.

JANET Sonny . . . be quiet!

SONNY We had one or two already, but I'm sure you'll
catch up fast.

FATHER What's going on in here?

SONNY It's a celebration, Father!

FATHER What's my liquor doing out? Who gave you
permission to go into my liquor cabinet?

(SONNY *takes out another glass and pours a shot*)

SONNY Here we are!

(*A pause*)

FATHER You opened my bourbon!

SONNY (*Holding his own drink*) Drink up, Father!

FATHER   What kind of hanky-panky is going on here?

SONNY   *(Waving his drink)* Come on! Down the hatch! You can finish those crackers later. *(Pause)* You're putting on a little weight as it is . . . you can do without cheese and crackers.

FATHER   *(Slams the plate on the cabinet counter)*   I don't want the goddamn cheese and crackers!

SONNY   You have to watch yourself, Father. You don't look so good to me. What do you think, Janet . . . how does he look to you? *(Pause)* I mean, a man as active as you've been can't mope about the house eating all day. Age can catch up to you fast. Take my word for it. You'll go to pot. I've seen it happen. You'll go to pot in no time. You don't want to end up like one of those overstuffed baboons you were telling me about.

FATHER   Why don't you shove it!

SONNY   Such language! And in front of Janet. In front of a pregnant woman.

JANET   Sonny!

> *(She grabs his arm to silence him. Pause.* FATHER *looks at one and then the other)*

FATHER   Pregnant?

SONNY   Yes. Janet's going to have a baby. A boy! I'm going

to be a father! (*Silence.* FATHER *stares at* JANET) Now what about that toast?

(*A pause*)

FATHER   She's pregnant?

SONNY   That's right. No feathers-and-cotton stuffing. I don't deal in that material. I deal in flesh and blood.

(FATHER *walks slowly to her, stands before her a moment, then slaps her across the face*)

FATHER   Whore!

(JANET *is stunned. She holds her face where she was slapped and then, suddenly, runs upstairs*)

SONNY   *Tch, tch, tch.* See what you did? You ruined the toast. (*Pause.* SONNY *holds his glass*) I thought you would be thrilled by the news. I was! I was overjoyed! I thought you would burst into song. (*Pause*) You know what you are, Father? You're nothing but a spoilsport. (*Finishes drink*) This is good bourbon, by the way. Fine stuff! (*Takes a cracker with cheese*) I think cheese and crackers go well with bourbon . . . don't you? (*Pause*) Well, I think I'll go wash up a bit.

(SONNY *goes up.* FATHER *stands where he is.* MOTHER *comes in*)

MOTHER   Did I hear Sonny's voice?

FATHER (*Slightly dazed*)   Yes.

MOTHER   Where is he?

FATHER   Upstairs.

MOTHER   Where's Janet?

FATHER (*Back to his old self*) How should I know! I
don't keep track of the goings on in this house!

(*He walks to the water jug*)

MOTHER   Father! Have you been drinking?

FATHER   No.

MOTHER   What are all the bottles doing out?

FATHER   I wouldn't know.

(*He goes to the cabinet and takes out a large glass.
He returns to the jug*)

MOTHER   Look at this mess! *Someone's* been drinking!
(*She starts to clean up, putting the bottles away, etc.*
FATHER *puts the glass down and tries to manipulate the
water jug with his one hand and arm*) What are you
trying to do?

FATHER   What does it look like?

MOTHER   You know that's impossible. You can't pick up
that jug with one hand.

FATHER   I'm thirsty!

MOTHER   Wait till Sonny comes down. He'll pour you a
glass.

FATHER   Oh no he won't! He's not pouring me anything!

MOTHER   I'll get you a cold drink then.

FATHER   I want my water!

MOTHER (*Leaving*)   I'll get you a cold glass of lemonade.

FATHER   I don't drink lemonade! I don't drink that sweet shit!

> (FATHER, *alone in the living room, awkwardly manipulates the jug.* SONNY *appears at the head of the steps. He carries his duffel bag over his shoulder. He watches* FATHER *a moment and then comes down and throws his bag onto the sofa*)

SONNY   Can I give you a hand, Father? (FATHER *ignores him.* MOTHER *comes in with lemonade*) I'd be more than happy to give you a hand.

> (*A pause*)

MOTHER   Let him give you a hand, Father.

FATHER   I don't need a hand!

SONNY   It would be much simpler if I gave you a hand.

FATHER   I'm not thirsty!

> (*He bangs the jug down and walks away*)

SONNY   You're sure you don't want a drink?

(FATHER *doesn't answer. He stands, facing away from* SONNY)

MOTHER (*Softly*) He wants one. Pour him a glass, Sonny. (SONNY *starts pouring.* FATHER *is still turned away*)

FATHER Don't pour me anything!

MOTHER Don't be so stubborn. You know you're thirsty.

FATHER I am not!

SONNY (*Holds out the glass to him*) Here.

(FATHER *doesn't turn. A pause.* MOTHER *puts the lemonade down and goes to her chair. She sees the duffel bag*)

SONNY If you don't want it, I'll drink it. (*He does*) I've developed a taste for the stuff myself.

MOTHER Isn't this your bag?

SONNY Yes . . . that's my duffel bag.

(*He comes over*)

MOTHER What is it doing on the sofa?

SONNY I'm leaving, Mother. I'm packing.

MOTHER You're packing?

SONNY Yes. Actually, I'm all packed. It's just my boots. (*He takes off his loafers and puts on his boots*) I really can't use loafers where I'm going.

MOTHER Why are you going?

SONNY I'm well rested now. In fact . . . I never felt better. I'm in my prime, as Father would say.

MOTHER I thought you were staying with us. I thought you would make this your home.

FATHER He's not needed here! One man's enough! He's not needed in this family!

MOTHER That's not true.

SONNY I'm afraid it is, Mother. Father knows what he's talking about. He knows I'm needed elsewhere. I mean, there's a war out there. I realize we're not fighting the Krauts any more . . . but the world is changing . . . the world is constantly changing. You have to keep up with the times, Father. From here on in it's the Chinks and those black sons of bitches. (*Has the boots on*) Ahhh, that feels better. I feel like myself again.

MOTHER At least stay for one more day.

SONNY I really can't.

MOTHER Stay for dinner then. There's a roast in the oven.

FATHER Let him go, for Christ sake!

MOTHER   It's so hot out. You're leaving at the height of the day.

SONNY   I'll manage. (*Pause. He picks up the loafers*) Do you mind if I take these with me? As a sort of keepsake? And they are a perfect fit! (*He unzips his bag and puts the loafers in*) Ronald certainly won't have need of them. He gave up the ghost! Ronald stopped eating. Can you imagine a thing like that? He had no desire to live! (*Pause*) It was to my advantage, of course. I ate his share of the food. Actually, there was only enough food for one of us. Only one of us could have come out of there alive.

> (SONNY *finishes packing. He zippers the bag.* JANET, *meanwhile, has appeared on the stairs*)

JANET   What's happening?

SONNY   (*Hoists his bag over his shoulder*)   Janet! I'm glad you came down. I was just saying good-by.

> (SONNY *walks slowly to the door, the duffel bag behind him, over his shoulder*)

JANET   (*Uncomprehensively*)   Goodby?

MOTHER   Sonny's leaving.

JANET   What about me?

MOTHER   What about you?

JANET   What about me! (*Runs after him and pulls at the bag*) You can't leave me like this!

SONNY Leave go.

MOTHER Janet!

JANET Take me with you.

MOTHER You'll hurt yourself.

JANET (*Pulling desperately*) I'll pack my bags!

MOTHER You can't go anywhere in your condition.

SONNY That's right, Janet. You're nine months pregnant. (*She pulls the bag off his shoulder. It falls to the floor*)

JANET I won't let you leave!

(*She drags the bag to the center of the room*)

MOTHER What's wrong with you?

(JANET *sits on the bag, holding each end with her hands. Silence*)

SONNY I think Janet's in labor.

MOTHER Labor?

SONNY Yes. That's where the problem lies. (*Pause*) Janet is about to have her baby!

(*He bends suddenly, pulling her legs up, throwing her back onto the bag*)

MOTHER What are you doing?

SONNY   Delivering the baby. (FATHER *runs at* SONNY, *with his good hand raised,* yelling, "AHHHHH!" SONNY *neatly sidesteps, tripping* FATHER *across the room, where he falls, moaning.* SONNY *pulls her legs over his shoulders*) This should have been an easy delivery. I didn't expect any problems. (SONNY's *hands are under her dress. She fights to get away*) Hold on, Janet! Grit your teeth! He's coming! (*He pulls the pink pillow out, holding it in the air triumphantly.* JANET *lies on the floor, crying.* FATHER *lies, moaning.* MOTHER *watches.* SONNY *gives the pillow a slap*) He's a healthy one, all right. He has a good color to him. (*He walks to* MOTHER *and hands her the pillow. She accepts it passively, standing silent*) Don't you think so, Mother? Don't you think he has a good color? (*Pause*) I'll open the shutters so you can get a better look at him. (SONNY *goes to the shutters and begins opening the slats*) This house can use the sun. It can use some of God's good sunlight. (*Opening the slats*) You'll be surprised. It'll do wonders. There's nothing like natural light. (JANET *and* FATHER *are standing. They watch* MOTHER *closely. She still stands passively, holding the pillow. As each set of louvers is opened, the sharp rays of the sun crisscross the room, silhouetting everything in it. The room takes on a new perspective. They are in a clearing, surrounded by the forest. This should not be a literal forest, but subliminal, suggested by the shapes and outlines of the furniture and objects at the edge of the room. We should never see beyond the shutters.* SONNY *adjusts the last louver*) There!

(*He turns and watches* MOTHER. *All three stand silently, watching her.* MOTHER *begins to rock the pillow in her arms. Then she hums*)

MOTHER (*Humming softly*) "Rock-a-bye baby, on the treetop, when the wind blows, the cradle will rock"— Such a sweet little boy. Such a soft little boy. (*She walks to the window and hums the rest of the stanza*) "When the bough breaks, the cradle will fall, down will come baby, cradle and all."

(FATHER *walks slowly to her*)

FATHER Mother? (*She hums the lullaby over and over, rocking the pillow*) Mother, do you hear me? (*Pause*) Mother?

(*Long pause.* JANET *goes to her*)

JANET Mother, I *am* pregnant. I'm really pregnant this time.

FATHER Do you hear her, Mother? Do you hear what she's saying?

JANET I'm pregnant, Mother. Feel me. Go ahead. You can touch me now.

(MOTHER *continues to hum and rock, oblivious to everyone.* FATHER *wanders away, leaving* JANET *there*)

FATHER (*To himself*) God, what did I do? What did I ever do? I loved the boy. We had our fallings-out, but I loved him. I cut his meat for him when he was small. I chopped it up into little pieces, tiny little pieces so it would be easy for him to digest.

(SONNY *walks to his bag and picks it up.* JANET *goes to him*)

JANET (*Softly*) You bastard! She never would have known the difference.

FATHER I'll need my rubdown tonight, Mother. Who's going to give me my rubdown?

(SONNY *walks across the room to the door*)

JANET You bastard! (*He opens the door. The sun shines through brightly.* JANET *walks halfway to him*) Take me with you, you bastard!

SONNY Sorry, Janet. I have to go. Father can tell you all about it. He fought in two of them. Two World Wars! I'm just beginning. I have my wars ahead of me. I have a lifetime ahead of me.

(FATHER *goes to* JANET *and tugs at her*)

FATHER You'll do it . . . won't you, Janet? You'll give me my rubdown!

JANET Get away from me! You're over the hill! (*Pushes him away and turns back to the door.* SONNY *has left*) SONNY! (*She walks slowly to the door, looks out into the hot sun, turns away, closes the door and clutches the folds of her dress. She leans against the door and speaks softly*) Don't leave me here. You bastard.

(FATHER *wanders around the room in a daze*)

FATHER What am I going to do tonight? What will I do? I have nobody to rub me down.

(*He finally sits in his rocker, moaning and rocking*

softly. MOTHER, *at the window, sings the full lullaby)*

MOTHER "Rock-a-bye baby, on the treetop, when the
wind blows, the cradle will rock, when the bough
breaks, the cradle will fall, down will come baby cradle
and all"—He's such a little bit of a thing . . . isn't he,
Father? And he looks just like Ronald. When he's a
little older you can take him to the beach and throw him
the ball. He's such a healthy little boy. That's a blessing.
That's a real blessing. I knew God would answer my
prayers. I don't think he'll ever be sick like Ronald . . .
although when Ronald was his age, when Ronald was
just a baby . . . he was healthy too. Do you remember,
Father? When he was four and five he was so strong,
he was such a healthy child . . . and then suddenly he
grew short of breath. Soon after Ronald's fifth birthday,
he developed a shortness of breath.

Curtain

Lyle Kessler was born in Philadelphia. While still a student he worked as a magician and escape artist, specializing in chain escapes.

Mr. Kessler appeared as Vladimir in the Philadelphia premiere of *Waiting for Godot*. In New York he studied with Lee Strasberg and worked as an actor in stock and off-Broadway. Later he turned to directing, and while looking for a play for his initial project in the Directors' Unit of the Actors Studio he decided to write his own, *The Viewing*, a one-act play he also directed for the ANTA Matinee Series, in 1967.

Mr. Kessler has been writing plays ever since, supporting himself by driving a cab, working as an assistant cameraman, teaching acting, and for two years directing blind actors in plays at the Guild for the Blind.

After completing his first full-length play, *The Watering Place*, Mr. Kessler was awarded a Rockefeller Foundation travel grant and will visit the theatre centers of Europe in 1969.

At present, he and his wife live in New York City.